FAR, FAR AWAY ON AN ISLAND CALLED ISLE ROYALE LIVED A CROW NAMED CHARLIE WHO ONE DAY DISCOVERED A DELICIOUS MYSTERY FOOD WITH HIS PAL, MOOOORIE. THIS DISCOVERY SET CHARLIE OFF ON AN ADVENTURE OF A LIFETIME AROUND THE UPPER PENINSULA OF MICHIGAN; MAKING NEW FRIENDS AND DISCOVERING A TRULY BEAUTIFUL LAND ALL WHILE LEARNING ABOUT THIS IRRESISTIBLE MEAL AND EVENTUALLY LEADING TO CHARLIE'S NICKNAME," CHARLIE 906".

CHARLIE: "HEY MOOOORIE, COME OVER HERE AND SEE WHAT I FOUND.

MOOOORIE: "HOLY WAH!! WHAT IS THAT? IT LOOKS AND SMELLS DELICIOUS!"

CHARLIE: "I DON'T KNOW, BUT I'M GOING TO DIVE RIGHT IN. FEEL FREE TO JOIN ME IF YOU WANT TO."

MOOOORIE: "I'M NOT GOING TO MOOSE OUT ON THIS FANTASTIC FIND. HA HA! YUM! YUM! YUM! YUM! YUM! YUM! YUM! YUM!"

ROCK HARBOR LIGHTHOUSE
AND THE RANGER III

MOOOORIE: " WAH! THAT WAS AMAZING. WHAT WAS IT? WHAT WAS IN IT? WHERE CAN WE GET MORE, MORE, MORE, MOOOOOOOORE?!?!"

CHARLIE: "MOOOORIE, I HAVE A FANTASTIC IDEA! DO YOU SEE THAT SHIP OVER THERE, THE RANGER 111? IT'S WHERE THAT AMAZING FOOD CAME FROM. SINCE I'M THE ONLY ONE WHO CAN LEAVE THE ISLAND RIGHT NOW, I WILL FOLLOW THAT SHIP TO FIND OUT WHAT IT IS, WHAT'S IN IT AND WHERE WE CAN GET MORE AND I PROMISE TO ANSWER ALL OF THESE QUESTIONS AND BRING YOU SOME BACK."

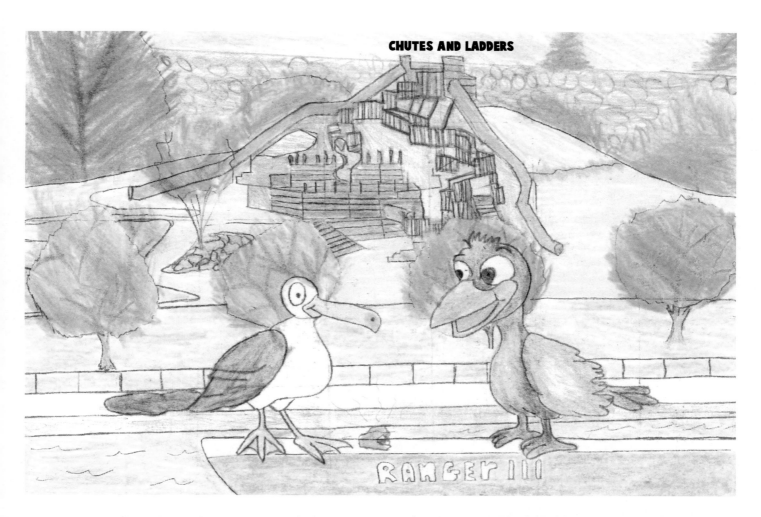

CHARLIE: "HI, MY NAME IS CHARLIE AND I AM ON A MISSION TO LEARN MORE ABOUT A TASTY MEAL THAT MY FRIEND AND I FOUND. BY THE LOOKS AND SMELLS OF WHAT YOU GOT THERE, IT IS EXACTLY WHAT I'VE BEEN LOOKING FOR. CAN I ASK WHAT IT IS AND WHAT'S IN IT?"

SCRAPS: "OH, WELL HELLO FRIEND. MY NAME IS SCRAPS AND THIS IS CALLED A PASTY. I KNOW THIS BECAUSE THEY MAKE THEM RIGHT DOWN THE STREET BUT I DON'T KNOW WHAT'S IN THEM BECAUSE I ONLY GET THROWN SCRAPS. I'D SHARE SOME WITH YOU BUT IT'S ALL MINE. MINE, MINE, MINE!"

CHARLIE: "OH, THAT'S FINE. THANK YOU, YOU HAVE ANSWERED A PIECE OF MY PUZZLE."

**HOUGHTON
HANCOCK**

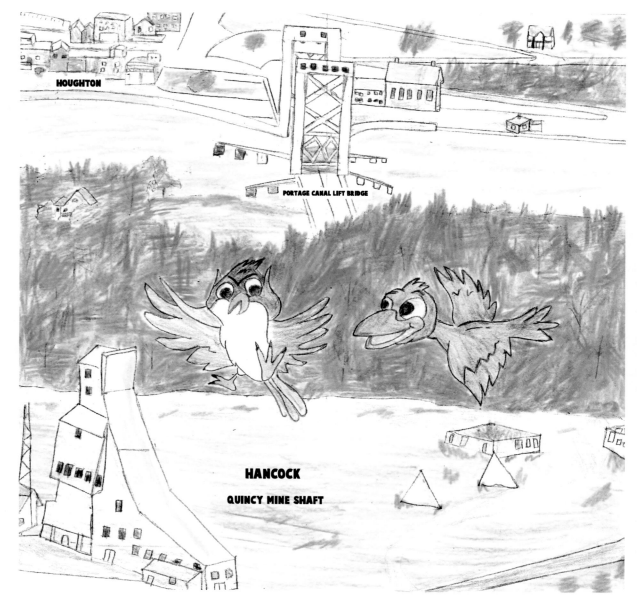

HOUGHTON

PORTAGE CANAL LIFT BRIDGE

HANCOCK

QUINCY MINE SHAFT

CHARLIE: "HEY THERE, I'M CHARLIE AND I'M ON A MISSION TO DISCOVER WHAT A PASTY IS. I WAS WONDERING IF YOU COULD TELL ME MORE ABOUT THEM?"

FALCO: "HI THERE, MY NAME IS FALCO. I CAN TELL YOU ABOUT A WEST COUNTRY, SCHOOLBOY, PLAYGROUND RHYME FROM THE 1940S. IT WAS ABOUT A PASTY AND IT WENT SOMETHING LIKE THIS: 'MATTHEW, MARK, LUKE, AND JOHN ATE A PASTY FIVE FEET LONG, BIT IT ONCE, BIT IT TWICE OH, MY LORD, IT'S FULL OF MICE' HA HA! MY FRIEND, SUSIE, WHO LIVES JUST NORTH OF HERE IN COPPER HARBOR CAN HELP YOU. YOU WILL FIND HER ON THE TOP OF BROCKWAY MOUNTAIN, JUST FOLLOW HIGHWAY 41 TO THE END."

BROCKWAY MOUNTAIN

CHARLIE: "HI. ARE YOU SUSIE? MY FRIEND, FALCO, SAID I COULD FIND YOU HERE AND THAT YOU MIGHT HELP ME FIND OUT WHAT'S IN A PASTY."

SUSIE: "YES, I AM SUSIE AND I CAN HELP YOU OUT. I KNOW THAT ONE OF THE INGREDIENTS IS DEFINITELY MEAT. I MET A FUNNY GUY DOWN AT THE JACOBSVILLE LIGHTHOUSE WHO MAY BE ABLE TO HELP YOU OUT SOME MORE, HIS NAME IS PHIL THE GOPHER."

CHARLIE: "HELLO, ARE YOU PHIL? MY NAME IS CHARLIE AND I HEARD YOU MIGHT BE ABLE TO HELP ME FIND OUT WHAT'S INSIDE THEM DELICIOUS PASTIES?"

PHIL: "YES, I AM PHIL AND I CAN DEFINITELY TELL YOU THAT THERE ARE ONIONS IN PASTIES. I COULD REALLY GO PHER A PASTY. HA HA! IF YOU WANT TO TRY TO FIND SOME, FOLLOW ME AROUND THE CORNER."

CHARLIE: "HOLY WAH! LOOK AT ALL OF THIS, IT'S LIKE PASTY PARADISE!"

PHIL: "YES SIR, DIG RIGHT IN! SOME DAYS IT RAINS PASTIES RIGHT HERE. AFTER YOU'VE HAD YOUR PHIL, HAHA, YOU SHOULD FLY OVER TO THE BISHOP BARAGA STATUE AND TALK TO MY FRIEND, CHIP."

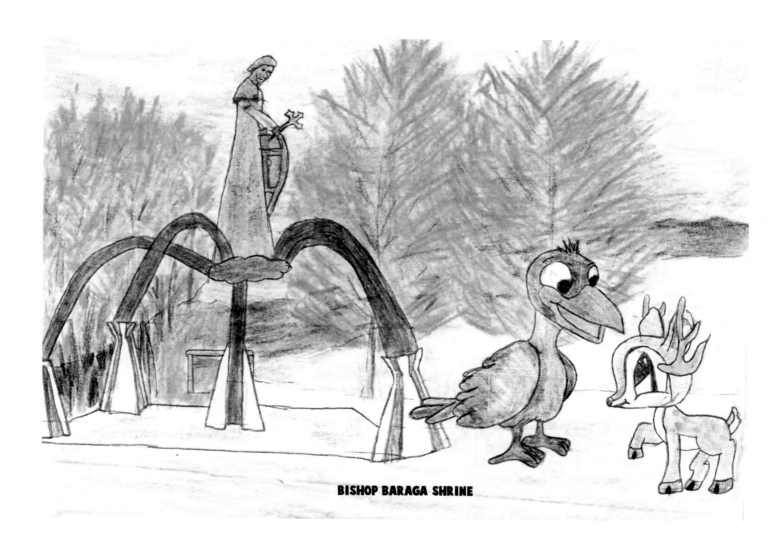

BISHOP BARAGA SHRINE

CHARLIE: "HI THERE, ARE YOU CHIP? MY NAME IS CHARLIE, AND PHIL TOLD ME THAT YOU MIGHT BE ABLE TO ASSIST ME IN FINDING OUT WHAT'S INSIDE A PASTY."

CHIP: "WELL, HELLO THERE. OH YES, THAT'S MY OLD BUDDY, PHIL, HE SURE IS FUNNY. YES, I CAN HELP YOU. MY FAVORITE FOOD IS ACTUALLY IN A PASTY; IT'S CALLED A TURNIP. IF YOU WANT MORE HELP, MY FRIEND ROBIN KNOWS A LOT ABOUT PASTIES; SHE IS ALSO MICHIGAN'S STATE BIRD, SO BE POLITE. TO FIND HER, JUST HEAD OVER THE HURON MOUNTAINS TO MARQUETTE."

MARQUETTE'S FORMER LOWER HARBOR ORE DOCK

CHARLIE: "HI, ARE YOU ROBIN? I'M CHARLIE AND A MUTUAL FRIEND, CHIP, SAYS THAT YOU MAY BE HELPFUL IN GETTING ME SOME INFORMATION ON A PASTY?"

ROBIN: "HI, CHARLIE. I DO HAVE SOME INFORMATION FOR YOU ON THE HISTORY OF PASTIES. THE PASTY CAME FROM CORNWALL, ENGLAND IN THE 1840S WHEN THE IMMIGRANT MINERS CAME HERE TO MINE FOR COPPER. THE PASTY WILL STAY WARM FOR UP TO EIGHT HOURS, WHICH MADE IT VERY PLEASANT TO HAVE DEEP IN THE MINES. IT WAS ALSO EASY FOR MINERS TO REHEAT ON A SHOVEL OVER A LAMP. CAN YOU BELIEVE THE EARLIEST KNOWN REFERENCE TO THE PASTY DATES BACK TO 1150 A.D.? THE PASTY HAS CREATED A CULTURE IDENTITY IN THE UPPER PENINSULA. YOU SHOULD HEAD OVER TO PICTURED ROCKS IN MUNISING TO SEE MY FRIEND, MYRTLE, FOR SOME MORE HELP.

PICTURED ROCK'S NATIONAL LAKESHORE

CHARLIE: "HEY THERE! ARE YOU MYRTLE? I'M CHARLIE AND OUR STATE BIRD, ROBIN, SAYS YOU MIGHT KNOW WHAT'S IN A PASTY?"

MYRTLE: "HI, MR. CHARLIE. OH YES, MS. ROBIN IS A GOOD FRIEND. WELL, CHARLIE, I KNOW THAT THERE ARE DEFINITELY POTATOES IN THEM PASTIES 'CAUSE I LOVE POTATOES. HEY, YOU SHOULD HEAD EAST OVER TO THE GREAT LAKES SHIPWRECK MUSEUM IN WHITEFISH POINT AND TALK TO MY FRIEND, HARE E. I BET HE KNOWS WHAT ELSE IS IN A PASTY."

LIGHTHOUSE AND GREAT LAKES
SHIPWRECK MUSEUM

CHARLIE: "HI, HARE E. I'M CHARLIE, A PAL OF OURS, MYRTLE, SAYS YOU MIGHT BE OF SOME HELP ON MY PASTY INFORMATION QUEST?"

HARE E: "HEY THERE, BUD. NOW, YOU CAME TO THE RIGHT PLACE BECAUSE I CAN TELL YOU THAT THERE ARE DELICIOUS CARROTS IN PASTIES. DID YOU KNOW CARROTS ARE HIGH IN VITAMIN A, WHICH IS ESSENTIAL FOR GOOD VISION? HEY! YOU SHOULD SEE YOUR WAY OVER TO SEE MY FRIEND, BANDIT, OVER BY THE GRAND HOTEL ON MACKINAC ISLAND. HE MIGHT HAVE SOME INSIGHT FOR YOU. HE HE!"

MACKINAC ISLAND'S
GRAND HOTEL

CHARLIE: "HEY, YOU MUST BE BANDIT. I'M CHARLIE AND HARE E SENT ME THIS WAY TO SEE WHAT YOU CAN TELL ME ABOUT PASTIES."

BANDIT: "HEY THERE, MISTER. WELL, DO I HAVE A FACT TO TELL YOU ABOUT PASTIES! DID YOU KNOW THAT THE WORLD'S LARGEST PASTY WAS MADE IN AUGUST 2010 IN CORNWALL, ENGLAND? WELL, IT MEASURED AT A CRAZY 15 FEET LONG AND WEIGHED A WHOPPING 1,900LBS AND THE COST TO MAKE IT WAS AN ESTIMATED $10,000. I WOULD HAVE LOVED TO SINK MY TEETH INTO SOME OF THE 1.75 MILLION CALORIES IT CONTAINED. HEY, I KNOW THIS SOUNDS EVEN CRAZIER BUT HEAD OVER TO NAUBINWAY TO SEE MY FRIEND, HUMPHREY THE CAMEL, FOR MORE INFORMATION."

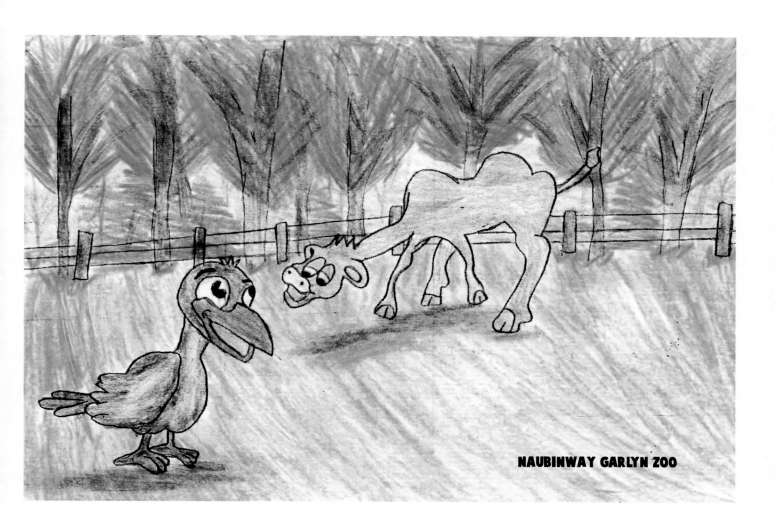

NAUBINWAY GARLYN ZOO

CHARLIE: "WELL, NOW, I'D BET ALL THE PASTIES IN THE WORLD THAT YOU'RE MR. HUMPHREY. I'M CHARLIE, A FRIEND OF BANDITS AND HE SAID YOU MIGHT BE ABLE TO HELP ME FIND OUT MORE ABOUT PASTIES."

HUMPHREY: "HEY, CHARLIE. YUP, YOU'RE RIGHT. WELL, I CAN TELL YOU WHERE I'M FROM THEY DON'T HAVE PASTIES. I AM SURE HAPPY I MOVED TO THIS LAND WITH YOU YOOPERS. I CAN TELL YOU THAT THERE IS A MAGNIFICENT CRUST ON PASTIES THAT I CAN'T GET ENOUGH OF. GO TALK TO MY FRIEND, HONEY, OVER IN MANISTIQUE; YOU'LL FIND HER NEXT TO THE WATER TOWER."

HISTORICAL
ROMAN STYLE
WATER TOWER

CHARLIE: "HEY THERE, HONEY. I'M CHARLIE AND HUMPHREY SAID I COULD FIND YOU HERE SO I COULD ASK YOU IF YOU KNOW ANYTHING ABOUT PASTIES."

HONEY: "HEY! YEAH, I CAN TELL YOU IF I HAD A PASTY RIGHT NOW, I'D BE A HAPPY CAMPER. DID YOU KNOW THAT IF YOU PUT KETCHUP ON A PASTY IT'S EVEN MORE DELICIOUS? YOU SHOULD TRY IT SOME TIME. HEY, I KNOW A CLEVER FELLOW WHO MIGHT KNOW A THING OR TWO ABOUT PASTIES; GO SEE KETTU OVER IN IRON MOUNTAIN BY THE CORNISH PUMP MUSEUM."

CORNISH PUMPING ENGINE AND MINING MUSEUM

CHARLIE: "HI! ARE YOU KETTU? I'M CHARLIE. HONEY SENT ME ON OVER YOUR WAY TO HOPEFULLY LEARN MORE ABOUT PASTIES"

KETTU: "HELLO! WELL, DO YOU BELIEVE IN SUPERSTITIONS? IF SO, LISTEN TO THIS... MINERS USED TO BELIEVE IN SPIRITS CALLED KNOCKERS. THEY WERE SAID TO CREATE KNOCKING SOUNDS TO EITHER INDICATE WHERE COPPER VEINS WERE OR THEY WOULD KNOCK TO WARN THE MINERS OF A POSSIBLE COLLAPSE. THEY DID THIS IN EXCHANGE FOR PASTY OFFERINGS LEFT BEHIND BY THE MINERS!" PRETTY FREAKY, RIGHT? HEY, HEAD OVER TO THE COPPER PEAK SKI JUMP IN IRONWOOD FOR SOME MORE INFORMATION FROM MY FRIEND, SPIKES."

COPPER PEAK
WORLD'S LARGEST
SKI FLYING JUMP

CHARLIE: "HELLO! YOU MUST BE SPIKES, I'M CHARLIE AND KETTU TELLS ME YOU MIGHT HAVE SOME INFORMATION ON PASTIES."

SPIKES: "WELL, I SURE DO. THE GRAVY TRAIN RUNS ALL OVER MY PASTY; THE MORE GRAVY THE HAPPIER I AM, YOU NEED TO TRY IT OUT. HEY, HEAD OVER TO AGATE BEACH STANTON PARK TO SEE MR. WHO, HE IS PRETTY KNOWLEDGEABLE."

AGATE BEACH

CHARLIE: "MR. WHO, I PRESUME? I'M CHARLIE AND SPIKES SENT ME TO HOPEFULLY GET ANY INFORMATION YOU MIGHT HAVE ABOUT PASTIES."

MR. WHO: "WHO? WHO ME? OH YES, FRIEND, I'LL TELL YOU WHAT... DID YOU KNOW THAT IN 1968, MICHIGAN DECLARED MAY 24TH NATIONAL PASTY DAY? IT'S MY SECOND FAVORITE DAY OF THE YEAR. OH, MY! THAT REMINDS ME, TODAY IS JUNE 25TH, MY FAVORITE DAY OF THE YEAR! THERE IS A PASTY FESTIVAL IN CALUMET. COME ON, LET'S GET GOING NOW..."

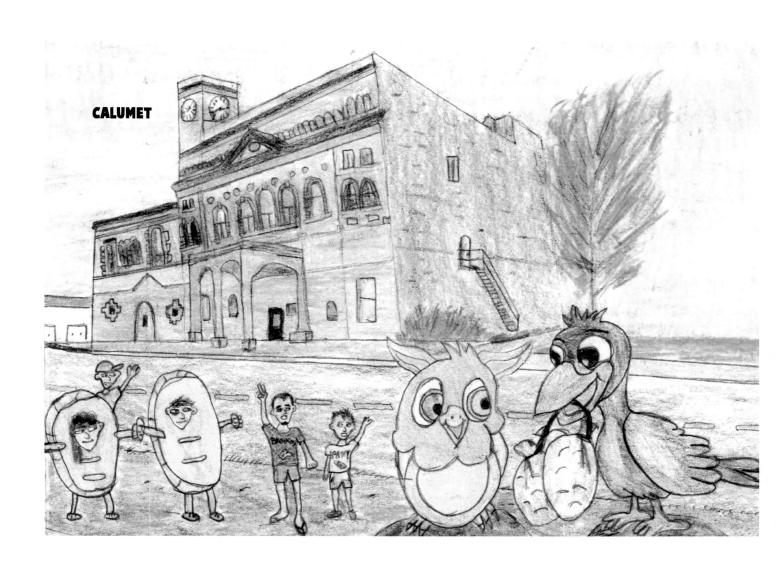

MR. WHO: "AAH, ANOTHER DAY IN PARADISE!!! WELL, SAFE TRAVELS HOME. AFTER THAT ADVENTURE AROUND THE UPPER PENINSULA, YOU'LL ALWAYS BE KNOWN AS CHARLIE 906."

AND SO, CHARLIE MADE IT HOME TO AN ELATED MOOOORIE; THEY STAYED UP FOR HOURS AND HOURS EATING PASTIES WHILE CHARLIE TOLD ALL OF HIS STORIES ABOUT HIS 906 ADVENTURES DISCOVERING THE DELICACY THEY CAME TO KNOW AS THE PASTY.

COLOR YOUR OWN

FALCO

MOOORIE

CHARLIE

SPIKES

BANDIT

MYRTLE

KETTU

HUMPHREY

906 CHARACTERS

Recipe For
Pasties
From Michigan's
Upper Peninsula & Charlie 906

Charlie 906

Cut shortening into flour and salt until mixture is coarse. Rub flour together in fingers to produce a coarse crumb. Add water and form into a ball. Divide into 6 equal rolled balls. Dust with flour, seal in plastic wrap. Chill 1 HR. Mix all the filing ingredients. Roll each dough ball on a lightly floured surface to a 9" circle. Add 1 1/2 C of filing to each. Fold pasty over to create a 1/2 moon shape. Seal the edges with a fork and cut 3 small slits on the top. Bake on a cookie sheet at 400 F for 45-50 min, until golden. Then Enjoy each Bite

Filling
* 1LB. Ground beef, 1LB Pork, 1/4"cubes
* 5 LG Potatoes, Peeled, 1/4" cubes
* 1 Small turnip, 1/4" cubes
* 1 1/2 LG onions, finely chopped
* 1 tbsp salt, 1 tbsp ground peper
* 2 Carrots, Peeled, 1/4" cubes

DOUGH
* 4 C. flour, sifted
* 2 tsp salt
* 1 1/2 C. shortening
* 10 tbsp ice water

71161902R00015

Made in the USA
Columbia, SC
25 May 2017